The Boston Tea Party

Angry Colonists Dump British Tea

Allison Stark Draper

The Rosen Publishing Group's
PowerKids Press™
New York

For my father

Published in 2001 by The Rosen Publishing Group, Inc.
29 East 21st Street, New York, NY 10010

First Edition

Book Design: Michael de Guzman

Photo Credits: pp. 4, 18 © 1998 North Wind Pictures; pp. 5, 7 © Archive Photos; p. 9 CORBIS/Bettmann; p. 10 CORBIS; p. 13 © Stock Montage/SuperStock; pp. 14, 17, 21 by MaryJane Wojciechowski.

Draper, Allison Stark.
    The Boston Tea Party : angry colonists dump British tea / by Allison Stark Draper.
        p. cm.— (Headlines from history)
    Includes index.
    Summary: Describes the series of events which led up to the Boston Tea Party and explains how this act helped bring about the war
for independence.
    ISBN 0-8239-5671-7 (lib. bdg.)
    1. Boston Tea Party, 1773—Juvenile literature. [1. Boston Tea Party, 1773. 2. United States—History—Revolution, 1775–1783—Causes]
I. Title. II. Series.

E215.7 .D73 2000   99-058708
973.2'7—dc21

Manufactured in the United States of America

Provided

by

Measure B

which was approved

by the voters in

November, 1998

CONTENTS

King George III Taxes
Americans to Pay for War

The colonists in America had to obey the laws of King George III.

4

Beginning in the 1600s, English men and women came to America to live in **colonies.** The **colonists** were **citizens** of England, but they had no say in the government. Many thought of themselves as more American than English.

The French had colonies in Canada, but they wanted more land. In 1754, the French attacked farms in

America. This started the French and Indian War. The American colonists went to war against the French and won.

The King of England at this time was George III. The king was glad the colonists had won the

The war between France and England was called the French and Indian War because the Indians helped the French fight against England.

war, but it had cost a lot of money. The king decided to **tax** the Americans to raise money. The Americans thought this was unfair. They had no say in how the English government was run. They did not want to pay English taxes.

5

Americans Smuggle in Tea to Avoid Paying Tax

In 1767, the English passed a tax on tea. Americans would have to pay three cents extra for each pound (454 g) of English tea they bought. Most Americans were not upset because they did not drink English tea. They drank tea **smuggled**, or brought in illegally, from Holland. In 1768, Englishmen who worked for the **customs** office in Massachusetts asked the English navy for help. They wanted the navy to stop the smugglers from coming into Boston. The English sent a warship with 50 cannons to Boston Harbor. The smugglers paid no attention to the warship.

In 1767, the English government passed a three-cents-a-pound tax on tea. ☜

7

Three Americans Killed in
Boston Massacre

The Americans did not want to pay taxes on things like paper, paint, and tea. They spoke out against the English, but the English kept on taxing them. On March 5, 1770, a fight broke out in Boston between angry Americans and English soldiers. This event was called the Boston **Massacre**.

The English became worried. They stopped taxing everything but tea. Few people drank tea, and the tax was very little. It looked like the Americans had won the fight against British taxes. Nothing had changed, though. The English still had the power to tax the Americans.

8

This picture shows American sailor Crispus Attucks being shot by British soldiers. 🖛

9

England Passes Special Act to Save One Tea Company

After 1770, most tea in America was brought in illegally. The Americans were no longer buying British tea. A trading company called the British East India Company had almost no money. In 1772,

10

it had 18 million pounds (8,165 tonnes) of unsold tea. In 1773, England passed a special tea act to save this company. The company could sell tea at a price that was less than the price of tea smuggled into America.

The British thought the Americans would be happy to drink tea that was cheap and legal. Instead the Americans were angry. They thought the Tea Act was a sneaky way of making them pay the tea tax. All British tea was taxed. If Americans bought tea from the British East India Company, they would be paying the tea tax.

This picture shows angry Americans forcing a British tea agent to drink tea. The Americans also put tar on him and rolled him around in feathers.

11

Samuel Adams Speaks Out Against Tea Act

Samuel Adams was an American **patriot**. He thought that by paying taxes the Americans were allowing the British to tell them what to do. Adams taught Americans that their opinions were important. He told them that they could take action to change unfair laws.

After the British passed the Tea Act in September of 1773, Adams found out that three British tea ships were heading for Boston. If the Americans paid the tax on the tea the ships were carrying, they would be saying that the British had a right to tax them. Adams wrote a letter saying that the

Tea Act was unfair. He sent the letter to the governor of Massachusetts. The governor was **loyal** to King George III of England. He paid no attention to Samuel Adams.

Samuel Adams told the colonists that they should fight to change unfair laws.

13

Samuel Adams Tries to Make Tea Agents Quit

Samuel Adams had a plan for ending the English tea trade into Boston. He wanted to make the British tea **agents** working in Boston quit their jobs. In other **ports** along the Atlantic Ocean, the Americans had forced the agents to quit. Tea shipments were returned to England or stored away.

Adams wanted the tea agents in Boston to quit in front of a crowd. If the Americans could force the tea agents to quit in public, it would show the British that the Americans had power over them.

Adams put up posters telling people to come watch the agents quit. The agents never came. The crowd was angry that the tea agents did not show up. Adams spent the next few weeks making speeches against the British government. Many Americans agreed with what Adams said.

Samuel Adams made many speeches against the British government.

15

American Soldiers Stop British Tea From Being Unloaded

The English tea ship *Dartmouth* docked in Boston Harbor in November of 1773. American soldiers kept the tea from being unloaded. King George III decided that on December 17, 1773, English customs officials could take the tea off the ship by force. Samuel Adams knew that the tea would end up in American stores. Americans would buy the tea and pay the tax on it.

Samuel Adams wanted to send the tea back to England. Other cities in America had sent back English tea. In South Carolina, the tea was stored away until 1776.

16

American soldiers stopped the tea ship Dartmouth *from unloading its tea.*

On December 16, 1773, Samuel Adams and 5,000 Americans asked the governor of Massachusetts to send back the tea. The governor took his orders from King George III. He would not send back the tea.

17

Chests of Tea Dumped Into Boston Harbor

Just after 6 o'clock in the evening on December 16, 1773, Samuel Adams and a group of patriots called the Sons of Liberty sneaked onto three British

18

tea ships. The ships were docked in Boston Harbor. Adams and his men dressed up as Native Americans so they would not be recognized.

When the men got on the ships, they locked the crews below. They smashed open 342 chests of tea. Each chest weighed 260 pounds (118 kg). They dumped the tea into Boston Harbor. When all the chests were empty, they swept the decks of the ships. They shook out their shoes to make sure no tea came onto the shore. The next morning, Adams sent men to **crush** any tea that had floated onto the beach.

Samuel Adams and the Sons of Liberty dumped 342 chests of tea into Boston Harbor.

19

Angry King George III Closes Boston Harbor

When he heard about what was later known as the Boston Tea Party, King George III was angry. He wanted the Americans to pay for the tea they had destroyed. He closed Boston Harbor and would not open it until the Americans paid back the money. The king sent 4,000 British soldiers to the harbor. He told the soldiers to keep ships carrying supplies out of Boston. He planned to **starve** the Bostonians until they obeyed him.

The British wanted to punish the Americans in Massachusetts. They also wanted to prove that England still

20 *British soldiers kept ships carrying supplies to the Americans out of Boston Harbor.*

ruled the American colonies. Americans in other colonies thought King George III was being too hard on the people of Boston. They sent food and other supplies by land so the Bostonians would not go hungry.

21

Boston Tea Party Is a Step Toward Independence

After the Boston Tea Party, other "tea parties" were held up and down the coast of the Atlantic Ocean. The American colonists wanted England to know that the American colonies were **united**.

The tea parties showed that many Americans did not want to be ruled by England. Americans respected patriots like Samuel Adams. They wanted to help the people of Boston when England closed Boston Harbor.

By helping each other and speaking out against England, the 13 colonies were taking a step toward independence. In time they would become a single, **unified** nation: The United States of America.

22

GLOSSARY

agents (AY-jents) People that act for another person or group.

citizens (SIH-tih-zens) People who are born in or who have the legal right to live in a certain country.

colonies (KAH-luh-neez) Areas in new countries where large groups of people move who are still ruled by the leaders and laws of their old country.

colonists (KAH-luh-nists) People who live in colonies.

crush (KRUSH) To destroy something by squeezing it hard.

customs (KUS-tumz) Taxes paid to a government on things brought in from a foreign country.

loyal (LOY-ul) Faithful to a person or idea.

massacre (MA-suh-ker) Killing a group of helpless or unarmed people.

patriot (PAY-tree-ut) A person who loves his or her country.

ports (PORTS) Cities or towns where ships come to dock and trade.

smuggled (SMUH-guld) Sneaked into the country illegally.

starve (STARV) To suffer or die from hunger.

tax (TAKS) Money that people give the government to help pay for public services.

unified (YOO-nih-fyd) Joined together.

united (yoo-NY-ted) Coming together to act as a single group.

I N D E X

W E B   S I T E S

To learn more about the Boston Tea Party, check out these Web sites:

http://www.historyplace.com/unitedstates/revolution/teaparty.htm
http://odur.let.rug.nl/~usa/E/teaparty/bostonxx.htm